Magic Spells
to
Get Your Fella

igloo

This book is published by Igloo Books Ltd
Henson Way, Telford Way Industrial Estate
Kettering, Northants, NN16 8PX
First published in 2004
© Copyright Smiling Faces Limited and Sevens Design 2004
All rights reserved
Printed in India

info@igloo-books.com

Warning: Not suitable for children
under 3 years, due to choking hazard.

This Magic Spells book is
full of Magical Chants to help
modern girls find and pull the
perfect man – not to mention
keep him! So if you want a little
Magic in your life, take this
book in your hand and read
aloud the Spells inside. We
can't guarantee your
success, but we wish you
lots of luck trying!

A Spell to
Make You
Irresistible

"With this Magic Spell I wish
To become a gorgeous irresistible dish,
Making everyone I meet
Fall in reverence at my feet.
Give me a well-toned body to flex
So I can pull the opposite sex."

A Spell for a Hot Date

"Desperate I am,
Desperate I be.
Find me a man who's perfect for me.
Make him rich,
Make him young.
Don't forget to make him well-hung."

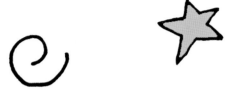

A Spell for a
Groovy Babe

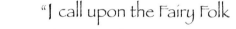

"I call upon the Fairy Folk
To use their wands in one Magic stroke.
To this gorgeous girl they'll grant
Three Wishes to use and enchant.
I wish for money, I wish for joy,
I wish for a handsome fit toy boy."

A Spell to
Get a Boyfriend

"I need some love and lots of attention,
Some TLC, and need I mention
Lots of fun both night and day,
And someone to cherish in every way."

A Spell to Make You a Great Dancer

"I call upon Fairy Magic to fall on my feet
As I step on the dance floor to a musical beat.
Keep me grooving like a disco diva,
Moving and raving with dancing fever."

A Spell for Bigger Boobs

"Alakazam, alakazear,
Make my flat chest disappear.
In its place put a large bust,
One I don't need to overly thrust.
Forget double D, forget double E,
Make them a whopping double G."

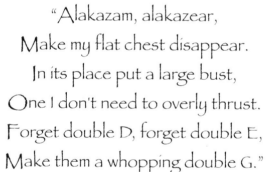

A Spell for
a Special
Makeover

"Past it I am,

Past it I be.

Make me young and

gorgeous to see.

No more wrinkles,

No more cares,

No more long unwanted hairs."

A Spell to Get Rid of Excess Body Hair

"Now I'm sprouting lots of hair
On my legs, my lip and everywhere.
I wish for a Spell to take it away
Before they go long, curly and grey.
Make me as smooth as a new born baby –
Not like a crock of over eighty."

A Spell to Make Food Slimming

"I call upon a Fairy's Magic Power
To fall on me in a shimmering shower.
Let me eat as much as I wish,
Emptying every delicious dish.
But as the next day doth come,
Keep me thin around my thighs and bum."

A Spell for
the Perfect Body

"I ask for just one Magical Wish,
To become the ultimate perfect dish.
Give me glowing hair and clear skin.
Give me a body that's beautifully slim.
Make me the object of others' desire,
No longer carrying an old spare tyre."

A Spell for Manageable Hair

"I'm sick of my hair being a bird's nest,
And never being able to look my best.
So with the power of Fairy Magic and luck
Give me a permanent perfect look.
No more knots, no more frizz,
Thanks to a Magical sparkle, fizz, bang, whizz."

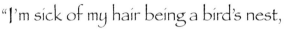

A Spell to Improve Droopy Boobs

"Floppy I am,
Floppy I be.
Make my boobs firm for me.
So make them pert,
Make them alert,
No longer hanging down to my skirt."

A Spell
to Stop You
Getting Older

"I call upon the Powers of Youth
To help me beat the ghastly truth.
No longer shall I become an old git,
Wearing slippers and drooling spit.
So keep me young and ever so sprightly,
Raving and grooving daily and nightly."

A Spell to Make
a Bum Smaller

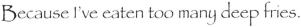

"Big is my bum,
Big are my thighs,
Because I've eaten too many deep fries.
Make this Magic work really hard
To take away my excess lard.
Make me trim, make me slim,
So I can give up the bloody gym."

A Spell
to Make a
Man Fitter

"My man has now let himself go,
Allowing his body to grow and grow.
So using the Magic in Fairy Wit,
Make him awake amazingly fit,
With massive pecs, a muscly back,
And the sexiest looking six-pack."

A Spell for a Perfect Kiss

"As I've kissed many a frog,
And found no Prince worth a snog,
Find me a man who is gorgeous and fit,
Who's up for a snog and a bit of crumpet.
Make it moist,
Make it long,
And make him wear a tiny thong."

A Spell to Get the Perfect Man

"Now I'm after a new man in my life,
So I can eventually become someone's wife,
I wish for a man who's hunky and cute,
Not some old-fashioned neanderthal brute.
Make him classy, make him romantic,
But most of all make his willy gigantic."

A Spell for the Perfect Tan

"As I am incredibly pale and white,
And go beetroot red in the merest sunlight,
I wish to develop the perfect tan,
To attract a gorgeous hunky man.
Make my skin all bronzed and brown,
So I can flash myself around town."

A Spell to Banish PMT

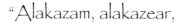

"Alakazam, alakazear,
Make my PMT disappear.
No longer do I want to be
A screaming loony banshee.
Make me lovely and full of fun,
Not wanting to tout a sub-machine gun."

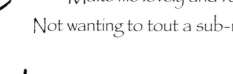

A Romance Spell

"On this Valentine's Day
I wish for a huge, beautiful bouquet.
Then perhaps as we dine
With fine food and expensive wine,
I can open a massive gift box
Hiding a diamond ring inside
some Belgian chocs."

A Spell to Improve Your Sex Life

"My sex life is now very sad,
And goes from dull to extremely bad.
So I call on the powers of debauchery
To make my life more of an orgy.
I'd like to swing from the chandelier
And use with style my God-given gear."

A Spell to Make You Look Sexy

"Next time I wear sexy underwear
I want my man to really stare.
Instead of flesh hanging over my panty line
I wish to look completely divine.
No more ripples,
No more spare tyre –
Just a figure to really admire."

A Spell to Find
Something to Wear

"What looked good in the shop last week
Now makes me look like a blobby freak.
So with the help of a Fairy's Magic
I wish for a wardrobe that is less tragic.
So next time I have an important date
There'll be no more over-short skirts
or a silly size eight.
Just clothes that are a perfect fit,
A stylish, stunning, contemporary outfit."

A Spell for a Thinner Waist

"Every time I look in my favourite mag
It makes me frown and want to gag,
As on each page I am always faced
With girls with hardly any waist.
So perhaps, just for a day,
This spell can take my spare tyre away."

A Spell to Make
the Perfect Man

"There are no perfect men who fit the bill,

Who are sexy, romantic and with no free will.

So with a pinch of Magic Dust I plan

To create the most perfect, gorgeous man,

Who will respond to my every

whim and command,

As well as sport an enormous gland."

A Spell for Revenge on a Love Rat

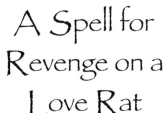

"I've discovered my man has cheated on me,
So all that's Magic hear my plea.
Make his willy only rise
When he's around other guys,
So all his days are filled with concern
As he starts to wonder if he's turned."

A Spell to Get Rid of Cellulite

"My legs look like ugly orange peel
So to all that's Magic I make this appeal.
Smooth out the skin on my legs and thighs,
So I can attract some gorgeous guys."